Dick Bruna

Miffy in the Snow

Big Tent Entertainment
New York

Miffy looked outside one day.

“Come and see!” she cried.

“It has been snowing all night long.

Please, may I go outside?”

The rooftops were all white with snow.

The school looked pretty, too.

But there would be no school today!

Miffy knew just what to do.

She put on her wooly hat.

Her boots were nice and warm.

With her scarf and gloves, she wore

a winter uniform!

First she found her yellow sled,

and pulled it up the hill.

Miffy slid down very fast,

it gave her such a thrill.

When she reached the big blue lake,

it had frozen through.

Miffy skated on the ice,

her favorite thing to do.

And she made a big snowman,

which took a lot of snow.

Miffy's mother came outside,

and clapped for her, "Bravo!"

But then they saw a little bird

sitting in the snow.

"Oh," he peeped. "How cold I am!

I have no place to go."

"Please don't feel sad," Miffy cried.

"This snow is not for you.

We'll build a nice warm birdhouse.

Yes, that's just what we will do."

So Miffy went back home to find

the things that she would need.

Miffy's mother came along

to get the bird some seed.

The two of them worked very hard

and built the house with care.

The bird seemed very happy

to sit high up in the air.

Then Miffy's mother turned to her,

"What a good job!" she said.

"But now we'd better go inside.

It's time to go to bed."

She took one last look outside

at all the snow and ice.

Miffy had such fun that day,

but her bed felt warm and nice!

Big Tent Entertainment
216 West 18th Street
New York, New York 10011

Originally published in 1963 as *nijntje in de sneeuw* by Mercis Publishing bv, Amsterdam, Netherlands.

Published in the U.S. in 2003 by Big Tent Entertainment, New York.
Publication licensed by Mercis Publishing bv, Amsterdam, through Big Tent Entertainment.

ISBN: 1-59226-041-1
Library of Congress Control Number: 2003091000

Printed in Germany.

10 9 8 7 6 5 4 3 2 1

NOGGIN